RETURN *of the* EXILED CHILD

THE WORKBOOK

Five Pathways IFS-Inspired, Workbook for Healing the Exiled Child

Companion to the book *Return of the Exiled Child: A Mindful Journey from Trauma to Wholeness*

BY
KEITH W. FIVESON

Work Mindfulness Institute™

Copyright © 2026 Keith W. Fiveson. All rights reserved.

No part of this Workbook may be reproduced, stored in a retrieval system, or transmitted in any form or by any means, including photocopying, recording, scanning, or electronic transmission, without prior written permission from the publisher, except for brief quotations used in reviews or professional training contexts with proper attribution.

Publisher: Work Mindfulness Institute™

ISBN: 978-1-7370818-4-5

Design and Layout: Andy Magee

This Workbook is intended for educational and personal development purposes.
It is not a substitute for psychotherapy, counseling, or medical care. Readers engaging in trauma or doing inner-child related parts work are encouraged to seek professional support when needed.

Printed in the United States of America.

Disclaimer

This workbook supports personal reflection and self-inquiry. It is not a substitute for professional medical, psychological, or psychiatric care. You should consult qualified professionals for any acute or ongoing mental health or medical concerns. All exercises are voluntary and should be approached at a pace that feels safe.

Scope of Use

The material in this workbook is designed to help you explore inner patterns, emotional imprints, and personal narratives. It provides structured guidance for self-understanding, not clinical intervention.

Internal Family Systems Note

Internal Family Systems is a registered trademark of the IFS Institute. Concepts referenced in this workbook are used for educational purposes. This workbook is not affiliated with or endorsed by the IFS Institute.

Trauma Sensitive Guidance

Some sections may evoke emotional responses. If you feel overwhelmed, pause, ground, or seek support from a trusted friend or professional. You are encouraged to work at a pace that respects your capacity and well-being.

Sources and Influences

This workbook draws from several disciplines that help you understand your story, build emotional literacy, and develop greater conscious awareness.

- **Archetypal psychology from Carl Jung.**
  You explore recurring patterns, inner figures, and symbolic themes that shaped how you learned to survive and relate.

- **Joseph Campbell's research on the monomyth.**
  You identify where you are in the universal path of challenge, descent, discovery, and return, and how this cycle operates in your life.

- **Narrative therapy principles.**
  You examine the stories you inherited, the roles you adopted, and the meanings you assigned to your experiences. You learn to externalize limiting narratives, reclaim authorship, and create language that reflects your truth rather than your conditioning.

- **Internal Family Systems concepts.**
  You study the inner parts that carry burdens, memories, and adaptive strategies. You learn how to meet these parts with curiosity and compassion so they can shift, soften, or release old roles.

- **Contemporary trauma research and somatic awareness.**
  You track sensations, impulses, and nervous system responses. You learn how stress and trauma shape perception, behavior, and emotional patterns.

- **Mindfulness based approaches.**
  You build present moment awareness so you can pause, sense, and respond with intention. You strengthen the capacity to stay regulated while engaging difficult memories or emotions.

- **The Consciousness Quotient Institute.**
  You draw from research on conscious experience, self-awareness, and cognitive-emotional integration. You learn how conscious states, reflective attention, and self-regulation support growth, clarity, and expanded perception.

These influences shape the structure and goals of this workbook. They help you understand your internal world, work with your stories, and integrate the parts of yourself that are ready to be seen, understood, and brought home.

Recommended Resources

These works provide useful context and further exploration:
- Richard C. Schwartz, *Internal Family Systems Therapy*
- Carl Jung, *The Archetypes, and the Collective Unconscious*
- Joseph Campbell, *The Hero with a Thousand Faces*
- Bessel van der Kolk, *The Body Keeps the Score*
- Gabor Maté, *In the Realm of Hungry Ghosts*
- Daniel Siegel, *The Developing Mind*

Dedication:

For everyone who has carried the weight of their story alone, and for those who are now ready to meet the parts of themselves they had to leave behind. This Workbook is offered in support of your effort to understand your past with honesty, to approach your internal world with steadiness, and to build a relationship with yourself that is grounded in compassion and clarity. May this process help you reclaim what was lost, soften what became rigid, and strengthen your capacity to live with greater coherence and connection.

This work is also dedicated to my wife, Charlotte, whose strength, insight, and presence have been essential throughout the development of this project. Her steadfast support, her capacity to reflect truth with care, and her belief in the value of this work continue to shape both the spirit and the integrity of this Workbook.

Table of Contents

Introduction: How to Use This Workbook 7

Pathway 1. Maps of Exile 30

Pathway 2. Wall of Armor 48

Pathway 3: Inner Sanctuary 56

Pathway 4. House of Mirrors 68

Pathway 5. The Journey Home 86

Appendix A: Facilitator Guide 105

Appendix B: Mini Glossary 111

Appendix C: Blank Tools and Maps 115

Introduction:
How to Use This Workbook

This Workbook provides a structured and supportive process for examining your personal history, understanding the origins of your adaptive patterns, and building the skills needed for integration. The exercises are designed to help you slow down, reflect, and engage with your internal experience in a clear, grounded way. You do not need to complete the Workbook quickly or in a linear fashion. You may move at a pace that feels manageable and return to sections as needed.

Each of the five Pathways mirrors the structure of the main book and offers a specific focus. Together, they guide you from early narrative exploration, through understanding your protective system, to developing internal safety, gaining clearer insight, and integrating the parts of you that have been disconnected. You will write, reflect, observe your body, and explore the beliefs and patterns that shaped your life story.

To use this Workbook effectively:

1. **Set aside regular time** for this work. Short, consistent sessions are often more supportive than long, intensive ones.
2. **Create a private and quiet space** where you can reflect without interruption.
3. **Approach each exercise with openness and curiosity.** You are not performing or producing anything for evaluation.
4. **Use the writing spaces fully.** Write freely and without editing. Follow your associations and allow details to emerge.
5. **Notice your body as you work.** Many insights arise through physical cues. Use the somatic sections to record these changes.
6. **Pause when needed.** If you feel overwhelmed, step back. Use the grounding practices, explained in the book, before continuing.
7. **Revisit sections** if new memories, patterns, or insights emerge.
8. **Seek support** when your emotional system signals that you need additional containment or guidance.

This Workbook is not intended to replace therapy or professional care. Instead, it acts as a companion that helps you build insight, compassion, and internal coherence. As you progress, you may discover unresolved narratives, protective behaviors, and vulnerable parts that need patient attention. Move steadily, remain honest, and allow your internal experience to become clearer over time.

You decide the pace. You decide the depth. The goal is clarity, connection, and integration—not perfection.

What to Expect Emotionally and Somatically

Engaging with your personal history and exploring unresolved experiences often brings emotional and physical responses that may feel unfamiliar, uncomfortable, or surprising. These responses are not signs of failure or regression. They are natural expressions of a system that is beginning to reveal long-standing patterns, beliefs, and protective strategies. Understanding what to expect can help you navigate this work with steadiness and clarity.

Emotional Responses

As you work through each Pathway, you may notice:

- **Shifts in mood**, including sadness, irritation, tenderness, or relief.
- **Waves of grief** connected to memories, unmet needs, or moments when you were unsupported.
- **Confusion or ambivalence**, especially when encountering memories that conflict with past narratives.
- **Increased self-awareness**, including recognition of how past experiences shaped beliefs, behaviors, and relational patterns.
- **Protective emotions**, such as anger, numbness, or defensiveness, which often emerge when deeper material begins to surface.
- **Moments of clarity**, where connections become evident and long-standing questions gain context.

These responses are indicators that your internal system is engaging with the material. Emotional intensity may rise and fall. Take breaks as needed and return when you feel prepared.

Somatic Responses

The body often registers experiences before the mind fully understands them. As you explore memories and protective patterns, you may observe:

- **Tension or constriction** in the chest, throat, stomach, or shoulders.
- **Changes in breathing**, such as shallow breaths during difficult memories or deeper breaths during moments of release.

- **Restlessness or fatigue**, which can signal activation or the need for restoration.
- **A sense of heaviness or lightness**, reflecting shifts in emotional load.
- **Tingling, warmth, or vibration**, particularly when contacting vulnerable or long-silenced parts.
- **Settling or softening**, as insights land and protective layers ease.

Somatic responses are valuable information. They help you track what parts of your story carry weight, where your system holds stress, and what brings relief or connection. Use the somatic reflection sections to record these cues, even if they seem vague.

Working With These Responses

Throughout the Workbook, you will be guided to:
- Notice changes without judgment.
- Slow down and ground yourself when intensity rises.
- Use breath and simple sensory practices to return to stability.
- Engage only with what feels manageable.
- Identify when a Protector is activated and pause to understand its concerns.

The goal is not to eliminate emotional or somatic responses but to build the capacity to observe, understand, and work with them in a supportive and contained way.

Expect this process to evolve. Some sections may feel easier than expected. Others may bring forward material that requires time and care. Both are normal. What matters is that you remain attentive, steady, and responsive to your own needs as you move through the work.

Safety and Regulation Guidelines

Engaging in traumainformed narrative work requires attention to safety, pacing, and internal regulation. These guidelines help you maintain stability as you move through difficult material and allow you to work with depth without becoming overwhelmed. Use these principles throughout the Workbook and return to them whenever you need to reestablish grounding or clarity.

Establishing a Stable Foundation

Before you begin a session, take a moment to orient yourself. Notice your surroundings, your breath, and your current emotional state. Check whether you feel present enough to work with reflective or challenging material. If you feel unsettled or activated, use a grounding practice before proceeding.

Working Within Your Window of Tolerance

Your mind and body have a natural range in which they can process material effectively. When you feel calm, focused, or slightly activated, you are within this range. When you feel overwhelmed, disconnected, or agitated, you may be outside it. If you notice you are moving

outside your window of tolerance, pause the exercise and use a breathing practice that helps you to feel stable. Resume only when you feel settled.

Recognizing Activation Signals

Pay attention to cues that indicate you are becoming dysregulated:
- rapid or shallow breathing
- increased heart rate
- difficulty focusing
- pressure in the chest or throat
- irritability, numbness, or emotional flooding
- a strong urge to stop, avoid, or push through

Activation does not mean you have done something wrong. It means your system needs support. Pause, ground yourself, and continue only when ready.

Using Grounding and Regulation Tools

Throughout this Workbook, grounding and somatic practices are provided to help you restore a sense of steadiness. These may include:
- slow, paced breathing.
- orienting to the room
- placing a hand on your chest or abdomen
- sensory grounding through touch, sound, or temperature
- brief pauses to stand, stretch, or walk.

These practices are not optional. They are essential tools for creating the internal conditions required to work with vulnerable parts of yourself.

Respecting Your Limits

This process is not a race. There is no benefit to pushing through difficult sections if your system is signaling discomfort or fatigue. It is appropriate to:
- stop midexercise and return later.
- revisit an earlier section for additional grounding.
- skip ahead to a regulation practice before continuing.
- complete the Workbook over weeks or months rather than days.

Respecting your limits is an important part of traumainformed work.

Maintaining Emotional Containment

After completing an exercise, take a few minutes to settle your system before returning to daily activities. This helps prevent emotional spillover. Consider ending each session with:
- a grounding practice.
- a few sentences describing your current state.
- a gentle physical reset such as walking or stretching.
- Protecting Your Privacy

INTRODUCTION: HOW TO USE THIS WORKBOOK

Keep your writing and reflections in a safe place. The clarity you develop depends on your ability to write without selfcensorship. Knowing that your work is protected creates the psychological safety required for honesty.

Working With Strong Reactions

If you encounter material that feels overwhelming or destabilizing, step back immediately. Do not force yourself to continue. Use grounding practices and consider reaching out to a trusted support person or a trained professional.

Honoring the Process

Safety is not the absence of discomfort. It is the ability to recognize what you are experiencing, respond to it effectively, and maintain connection with yourself as you work. These guidelines help you stay oriented, regulated, and supported as you move through the deeper layers of your story.

When to Seek Outside Support

This Workbook invites you to engage with memories, emotions, and internal patterns that may have remained hidden or unexamined for years. While the exercises are designed to be grounded and contained, working with unresolved material can sometimes activate emotional or somatic responses that exceed your current capacity. Seeking outside support is a strength, not a setback. It reflects an understanding that healing is both an internal and relational process.

You may benefit from additional support if you notice any of the following:

- **Persistent Overwhelm or Emotional Flooding**
  If you find that you are consistently unable to stay within your window of tolerance, or if emotional waves feel unmanageable, a therapist or counselor can help you establish safety and pacing. This is especially important if you experience panic, persistent fear, or dissociation.

- **Difficulty Regulating Physical Responses**
  If your body reacts strongly during exercises—for example through rapid heartbeat, shaking, numbness, or chest tightness—and these sensations do not settle with grounding practices, professional guidance can help you work with these responses more safely.

- **Unclear or Conflicting Memories**
  As you explore your story, memories may surface that feel confusing, contradictory, or fragmented. A trauma-informed clinician can help you sort through these experiences without forcing clarity or creating further distress.

- **Intensified Protective Patterns**
  If you notice increased avoidance, irritability, detachment, overworking, perfectionism, or compulsive behaviors, these may indicate that protectors are working harder than usual. Support can help you understand these patterns without increasing internal conflict.

- **Emergence of New or Long-Suppressed Material**
  If you encounter memories or emotional themes you have never explored before, or if material surfaces that feels larger than what you can manage on your own, working with a trained practitioner offers containment and skilled guidance.

- **Interference With Daily Life**
  If your ability to function at work, in relationships, or in day-to-day activities becomes compromised, pausing the Workbook and seeking support can help stabilize your system.

- **History of Complex Trauma or Dissociation**
  If you have a known history of complex trauma, dissociation, or long-term emotional suppression, additional support is recommended while using this Workbook to ensure your process remains safe and grounded.

- **Sudden Changes in Mood or Behavior**
  If you experience significant changes in sleep, appetite, mood, or energy that persist for more than a few days, consult with a therapist or healthcare provider.

- **Suicidal Thoughts or Self-Harm Urges**
  If you experience thoughts of harming yourself or others, or if any urges toward self-harm arise, stop immediately and seek emergency or crisis support. Use the crisis resources available in your region.

- **Support as a Collaborative Resource**
  Seeking outside support does not mean you cannot continue this work. Many people benefit from exploring the Workbook alongside therapy, coaching, or somatic work. A skilled professional can help you deepen insights, regulate your system, and integrate experiences in a contained and supportive environment.

The goal of this Workbook is to help you understand your story with clarity and compassion. Knowing when to reach for support is an essential part of honoring that intention.

Section I.
Foundations

The Purpose of This Workbook

This Workbook gives you a structured process to examine your history, understand your internal system, and strengthen your capacity for integration. Many people move through life carrying unresolved experiences that continue to shape their thoughts, behaviors, and relationships. These experiences may not be fully conscious, yet they influence patterns such as avoidance, perfectionism, emotional distancing, over-functioning, or chronic self-doubt.

The purpose of this Workbook is to help you identify and understand these forces with clarity. You will explore the origins of your beliefs, the conditions that shaped your nervous system, and the parts of you that have worked tirelessly to protect your vulnerability. This process allows you to see your story in a more coherent and compassionate way. As you develop insight and awareness, you gain the ability to make choices that are grounded rather than reactive. The intention is not to relive old pain, but to create the conditions for a more fully integrated self.

Understanding the Five Pathways

The Workbook follows the same five Pathways introduced in the main book. Each Pathway highlights a different aspect of your inner system and offers exercises that build on one another.

Pathway 1, Maps of Exile, explores the early experiences and formative moments that shaped your internal narrative. You identify the origins of your Exiled parts and the unmet needs or emotional burdens they carry.

Pathway 2, Wall of Armor, examines the defenses you built to protect your vulnerability. You study your Protectors, Managers, and adaptive strategies to understand how they developed and what they continue to guard.

Pathway 3, Inner Sanctuary, focuses on developing safety, regulation, and internal capacity. You learn practices that help you contact Exiled parts without overwhelm, and you strengthen the ability to remain present with your emotional experience.

Pathway 4, House of Mirrors, helps you identify distortions, learned beliefs, inherited narratives, and ways of seeing yourself that may no longer serve you. You examine the stories that shaped your identity and the emotional patterns that formed around them.

Pathway 5, Journey Home, integrates the insights and experiences from the previous Pathways. You reconnect with your Exiled Child, form new internal relationships, and clarify the commitments and practices that support continued growth.

Understanding these Pathways helps you navigate the Workbook with intention and gives you a clear sense of progression.

Your Commitment to the Work

This kind of reflective work benefits from consistency, patience, and a willingness to stay connected to your internal experience. The Workbook is effective when you:

- approach the exercises with openness and honesty.
- allow yourself to slow down and reflect without rushing.
- track your emotional and somatic responses as they arise.
- recognize when protectors emerge and explore their purpose compassionately.
- take breaks when you feel overwhelmed or fatigued.
- return to sections when new memories or insights surface

You set the pace. The goal is steady engagement, not perfection or completion under pressure. This commitment is a commitment to yourself: to understand your history, to meet all parts of you with care, and to build the internal capacity needed for integration.

Preparing Your Inner and Outer Space

Your environment and internal state influence how deeply and safely you can engage with this material. Before starting each session, take time to prepare both.

Outer space: Choose a quiet, private location where you feel comfortable writing and reflecting. Minimize interruptions. Keep a notebook or additional paper nearby if you need more room for writing. Consider having water, a blanket, or grounding objects available.

Inner space: Begin each session by checking in with yourself. Notice your breath, your body, and your current emotional state. Identify whether you feel settled enough to proceed. If you feel scattered, activated, or tense, use a grounding practice from the Inner Sanctuary Pathway before continuing.

Establish a rhythm that supports you. Some people use a brief centering practice before writing; others take a few minutes to settle afterward. What matters is that you create continuity and stability as you move through the exercises.

This section provides the foundation for the work ahead. Each Pathway builds on these principles to help you move toward clarity, compassion, and integration.

Entering Pathway 1:
Beginning the Work

You are now ready to start Pathway 1. This is where you begin looking at your own story with clarity. Before you move into the exercises, it helps to understand why this first step matters.

Your early experiences shaped how you see yourself, how you relate to others, and how you manage stress and uncertainty. Some of these experiences were stable and supportive. Others were confusing, painful, or inconsistent. You adapted to all of them. You learned what kept you safe, what brought approval, and what reduced conflict. Over time, those adaptations became automatic. You may still use them today even when the original conditions are no longer present.

Pathway 1 helps you examine these early influences without judgment. You identify the people, places, events, and messages that shaped your beliefs, emotions, and behaviors. You look at the situations where you felt unseen or unsupported, and you track the adjustments you made to navigate those moments. You approach this work with the understanding that your adaptations were intelligent responses to the circumstances you lived in.

The purpose of this Pathway is not to relive old pain. It is to develop a clear and accurate map of what shaped you. When you can see the origins of your patterns, you can work with them instead of being directed by them. You gain more insight into why certain parts of you react the way they do. You begin to understand the younger parts of yourself that still carry unmet needs or unresolved emotions.

This section of the Workbook supports you in:
- identifying the early conditions that influenced your development
- recognizing the messages you absorbed from family, culture, and environment
- naming the roles and personas you adopted to stay safe or connected
- mapping the parts of your internal system that formed during those years
- understanding how these patterns continue to show up in your adult life

This work requires steadiness and curiosity. You do not rush through it. You give yourself time to think, feel, and remember. You stay grounded in the present while looking at the past. The prompts in Pathway 1 help you focus, stay organized, and move through your story in a contained way.

By the end of this Pathway, you will have a clearer view of where your internal landscape began. This prepares you for the next step, where you explore the strategies, defenses, and protective roles that grew from these early experiences.

You are starting at the beginning of your story.

This is where understanding takes root.

Our Inner Cast of Characters

A Guide for Your Journey

Every person carries an inner cast of characters that holds memories, emotions, instincts, and protective strategies shaped by lived experience. These characters influence the patterns you repeat, the reactions you have, and the ways you relate to yourself and others. This Workbook introduces the primary characters you will meet on your journey. They may appear through your thoughts, sensations, beliefs, or behaviors. You do not need to search for them or force anything to happen. Each part will reveal itself in its own time, and your role is to approach whatever arises with curiosity, clarity, and compassion.

These characters belong to three core systems: the Self System, the Manager System, and the Firefighter System. Together they work to protect the Inner Child and the deeper Orphan, and they all respond to the influence of the Shadow. You are not attempting to eliminate any character or silence any voice. You are learning how to recognize them, understand their purpose, and relate to them from your True Self.

Internal Family Systems describes how these parts developed specific roles to help you manage pain, navigate relationships, and survive difficulty. Jungian psychology views them as archetypes that express universal patterns of human experience. Joseph Campbell's Hero's Journey frames them as guides, protectors, challengers, and messengers who accompany the hero through critical thresholds and moments of change. Narrative Therapy emphasizes that each character carries a story shaped by your history, and that these stories can be explored and rewritten in ways that support healing and freedom.

Welcoming all of these characters allows you to see your inner world with greater understanding. As you get to know them, you will recognize how some have worked to keep you safe, how others have pushed you forward, and how a few have been holding pain you were not ready to feel. When you relate to these parts from your True Self, you bring steadiness, compassion, and leadership to your internal system.

The illustration on the next page offers a visual introduction to many of the characters you may encounter. You may not see all of them immediately, and that is entirely natural. Your task is simply to meet what shows up, listen with openness, and allow each character the space to speak in its own way.

As you begin this work, remember that every part in your Inner Cast has played a meaningful role in your survival and development. Understanding them more deeply allows you to

form a new relationship with your internal world, one that supports clarity, connection, and healing. This is the foundation for the journey ahead.

Figure 1 - Source -IFS, Jung, Campbell

How to Use This Image

This visual introduces the various character roles used throughout the Workbook. You may recognize parts of yourself or see how these figures appeared for you in relationships, as you work through the exercises. Please bookmark the image, to refer to it to help you recognize patterns, reactions, and internal strategies. These characters are not diagnoses. They are adaptive roles that developed in response to your history.

Each character belongs to one of three internal systems:

Self-System
Represents your core awareness, stability, and ability to lead your internal world.

Manager System
Represents the proactive strategies you use to stay in control, stay safe, and reduce emotional discomfort before problems arise.

Firefighter System
Represents the reactive strategies that appear when you feel overwhelmed or triggered and need immediate relief.

Exiles
Represents the younger, vulnerable parts of you that carry early pain, unmet needs, shame, fear, or emotional burdens. These parts require patience and care.

The characters shown in this illustration are examples. You may recognize some immediately. Others may emerge over time as you work through the Pathways.

You are not expected to match your experience perfectly to each figure.

Use the image as a reference point for noticing:

- what role a part is playing
- how that part protects you
- how that part learned its job
- what that part is trying to prevent
- what that part still believes about your safety and your worth

You may rename the characters or identify new ones that better match your internal experience. What matters is that you understand the function and intention of each part.

This image is a map. Your internal system is unique.

Use the characters as guides, not rules.

The Three Internal Systems (Integrative Model)

You can think of your internal landscape as three interacting systems. These systems are not rigid categories. They overlap and speak to each other. They shift depending on stress, safety, and context. This model draws from Jungian psychology, trauma theory, somatic awareness, and modern parts work.

1. The Self System

Your core awareness.
Your steady center.
Your capacity for presence and leadership.

The Self System includes:

True Self

Calm, clear, curious, compassionate. Holds the wisdom to lead your internal world without force.

Inner Child

Carries original sensitivity, emotional truth, vulnerability, and unmet needs. Remembers what hurt and what was missing.

Orphan / Abandoned Child

Holds deeper layers of loneliness, loss, and disconnection. Protects you by withdrawing or numbing.

Shadow

Holds the emotions, impulses, memories, and truths exiled from consciousness. Emerges when your system is overwhelmed or when truth must surface.

The Self System is the foundation for healing.

Everything in this Workbook helps you strengthen its presence.

2. The Manager System

Your long-term protectors.
The strategies that maintain control, order, and predictability.
Managers keep life organized, so you do not feel overwhelmed. They look ahead, anticipate danger, and try to prevent pain.

Common Manager archetypes include:

Controller

Keeps things structured to prevent mistakes or emotional exposure.

Pleaser

Maintains harmony, connection, and approval to avoid conflict or rejection.

Strategist / Analyst

Solves problems through planning, logic, and thinking ahead.

Critic / Judge

Monitors behavior through pressure, standards, and self-judgment to avoid shame or failure.
Managers are proactive.
They prevent emotional intensity by keeping life tightly managed.

3. The Firefighter System

Your emergency responders.
The parts that react quickly when emotional pain breaks through.
Firefighters move fast to reduce overwhelm. They are not thinking about the future. They are trying to stop the internal fire *right now*.

Common Firefighter archetypes include:

Firefighter

Acts urgently to shut down rising emotion.

Avoider

Pulls away, numbs, disconnects, or withdraws when things feel too intense.

Distractor

Creates movement, stimulation, or escape to avoid stillness and sensation.

Reactor

Uses intensity, anger, or force when the system feels cornered.
Firefighters are reactive.
They show up when the internal system senses danger or overwhelm.

How to Use This Inner Cast in the Workbook

Do not use these archetypes to label yourself. Use them instead to understand the energetic forces within you, that drive your behaviors.

Throughout the Workbook you will:
- Identify which inner figures shaped your early life.
- Notice how they show up in relationships, decisions, and patterns.
- Understand the fears, beliefs, and protective roles behind each part.
- Recognize how these systems influence your body and emotions.
- Learn to listen without merging or losing clarity.
- Rebuild a trusting relationship between Self and the inner cast.
- Offer new roles so old patterns can soften.

The aim is simple and achievable:

You lead your system from your True Self.

You meet each part with respect and curiosity.

You integrate what was once fragmented.

You reclaim the child inside who was left behind.

This is the beginning of your journey inward.
This is where your story begins.

Lighting the Way
Entering the Work

The Spiral and Your Breath

It's important to prepare yourself for the trip ahead. It takes a great deal of work to go deep, to excavate the inner sanctuary, to remember, disrupt, reclaim, and return, but this is the journey of life. As we begin this workbook, it is important to be prepared for the deeper work ahead. So, we start with the Spiral to lift up the science of the breath, to show you how it becomes your first and primary guide on a challenging but meaningful journey. This section also introduces the arc of the Hero's Journey in a simple, accessible way so you can understand the path you are stepping onto without feeling overwhelmed.

The Role of Spiritus and Breath

Breath has been recognized across cultures as the bridge between body and awareness. When you slow your breathing, you influence your vagus nerve, calm your autonomic nervous system, and create a foundation of safety. You do this before any memory work. You do this before you engage any difficult material.

You use the Spiral as a visual cue to support this process. Inhale as the Spiral widens. Exhale as it narrows. This rhythm helps stabilize your mind. It anchors you in the present. It reduces reactivity. It prepares you for the emotional and psychological work ahead.

Clinical Applications of Respiration

Controlled respiration stabilizes your physiology. Clinical studies show that intentional breathwork supports:

- Higher heart rate variability, which reflects improved resilience.
- Increased vagal tone, which helps regulate emotions.
- Reduced amygdala activation, which reduces fear responses.
- Better prefrontal function, which enhances reflection and clarity.

These shifts are not abstract. You feel them. You notice your pulse slow. You sense your body soften. You experience more room inside yourself. This makes it possible to approach complex memories with steadiness.

Autonomic Nervous System Regulation

Trauma often leaves your autonomic system organized around defense. You may overreact to small triggers. You may feel numb, tense, or hypervigilant. Breathwork interrupts these patterns. Each slow exhale signals safety. It tells your system that it can reduce its protective stance.

You create a physiology that supports curiosity. You lower the intensity of emotional charge. You make room for insight.

The Hero's Journey as a Map for Your Work

The Hero's Journey offers a practical way to understand the inner process you are about to enter. Joseph Campbell studied stories from cultures across the world and found a shared pattern in how human beings move through struggle, discovery, and return. Although the images and symbols differ, the underlying structure is the same. A person begins in a familiar state, receives a call to face something unsettling or long avoided, crosses into unfamiliar territory, experiences challenges or inner conflict, and eventually emerges with a new understanding of themselves. This pattern appears because it reflects a psychological truth. Transformation has a shape.

Carl Jung described a similar movement in his work on individuation. He observed that healing and development require meeting the parts of oneself that were ignored, split off, or hidden. Myths, dreams, and religious narratives all mirror this internal journey. They describe a person confronting their fears, wrestling with their shadow, discovering new capacities, and returning to their life with greater insight and responsibility. Whether you look through the lens of psychology, spirituality, or narrative, the arc is consistent. Growth follows recognizable steps. When you understand those steps, your own process becomes easier to navigate.

As you move through this Workbook, you will see parallels between your experience and the stages on the map. You may resist the call to look inward. You may feel uncertain before crossing the threshold into deeper work. You may meet inner protectors who function like mentors, trying to keep you safe. You may enter a more challenging phase where the patterns you carried for years become more visible. None of this signals failure. These moments simply show that you are inside the terrain where meaningful change happens. When you begin to integrate what you discover, you return to your ordinary life with a clearer sense of yourself and more freedom in how you respond to your world.

The Hero's Journey is not included here as a symbolic story. It serves as a structure that helps you orient yourself. Many people become discouraged when they feel lost or confused during inner work. This map shows that these experiences belong to the process. They are predictable, navigable, and shared. You are not outside the pattern. You are inside it.

ENTERING PATHWAY 1: BEGINNING THE WORK

[Diagram: The Hero's Journey cycle showing — ASCENT TO A HIGHER PLANE, END?, RETURN WITH SPECIAL KNOWLEDGE, STASIS, BEGIN, CALL FOR ADVENTURE, MASTER OF TWO WORLDS, REFUSAL OF THE CALL, ROAD BACK HOME, MEETING THE MENTOR, THE ORDINARY WORLD, THE NON-ORDINARY WORLD, REFUSAL OF THE RETURN, CROSSING THE THRESHOLD, THE ULTIMATE BOON, TEST ALLIES AND ENEMIES, THE ORDEAL IN THE ABYSS / FACING THE SHADOW SELF]

THE HEROIC JOURNEY INTERPERTATION

Prompts for Your Blank Journey Map

Later in this Workbook you will find a blank version of the Hero's Journey diagram (Page 119). Use it to track your path through this work. This exercise turns the map into a personal tool rather than an abstract concept.

The following prompts will help you fill in your own journey:

1. **Your Ordinary World**
   Describe the conditions of your current life. Note your routines, relationships, stresses, and patterns. What feels familiar, stable, or repetitive? What keeps you anchored?

2. **The Call for Change**
   Identify what is inviting you to look inward. This may be a symptom, a conflict, a transition, a memory, or a sense that something is no longer sustainable.

3. **The Initial Resistance**
   Name the reasons you hesitate. Consider beliefs, fears, protectors, or stories that hold you back from moving toward deeper work.

4. **Crossing the Threshold**
   Describe one moment, decision, or realization that brought you into this process. It does not need to be dramatic. It only needs to be true.

5. **Allies, Mentors, and Supports**
   List the inner or outer resources that help you move forward. These may include people, practices, parts of yourself, or insights that stabilize you.

6. **Challenges, Patterns, and Tests**
   Identify the internal and external challenges you face as you go deeper. Consider the behaviors, beliefs, or parts that show up during this phase.

7. **The Ordeal or Abyss**
   Reflect on the most difficult material you have encountered so far. This may include memories, somatic reactions, emotional patterns, or long-held narratives.

8. **What You Are Learning**
   Describe the insights, strengths, or understandings emerging as you work with these experiences. Note any shifts in awareness or behavior.

9. **The Return**
   Consider how you are bringing what you learn back into your daily life. Identify concrete changes in how you relate to yourself or others.

These prompts guide the reader without forcing interpretation. They help them see the structure of their work, place themselves within the arc, and recognize progress even when the experience feels unclear.

Working with Memory Safely

This Workbook does not ask you to revisit trauma without preparation. It gives you tools to stay grounded while exploring difficult experiences. You use breath to stay within your window of tolerance. You take breaks when your system signals fatigue. You reach out for professional support when needed.

The goal is not to relive pain. The goal is to create enough safety to understand your story.

Medicine-Assisted Trauma Work (Optional and Regulated)

Some people work with regulated therapies such as low-dose ketamine MDMA-assisted therapy, or cannabis microdosing under clinical supervision. These approaches can reduce fear responses, support emotional access, and enhance integration. They require a licensed clinician, a safe environment, and a clear therapeutic plan.

*This Workbook does not promote unsupervised medicine use. It acknowledges that regulated approaches exist and can be part of a broader healing plan and that each individual has to decide what is right for themselves.

How to Use the Practice Pages

You will find open spaces and writing lines included throughout the workbook. Please use these pages to record:
- What you feel in your body during breath practice.
- Thoughts, images, or memories that surface.
- Emotional shifts that occur.
- Any internal signals to pause.

These reflections help you track your process with clarity. You do not need this workbook to record reflections, it is recommended though. Keep a focus on your body, mind, breath, food, sleep, relationships, environment, and emotions and energy all of the time.

Your First Practice

Sit comfortably. Bring your attention to the Spiral. Inhale as it opens. Exhale as it narrows. Complete five rounds.

Notice how your body responds. Notice your state of mind. Notice if you feel more present.

This is your first step on your own Hero's Journey.

MAP OF EXILE

"Every exile begins with forgetting the moment we lose the sound of our own voice. To return, we must first trace the map of where we vanished."
— KEITH W. FIVESON

Pathway 1. Maps of Exile

LEARNING OUTCOMES:

- Identify early experiences that shaped your first Exile.
- Describe the emotional imprints you still carry.
- Notice the patterns that formed around unmet needs.
- Clarify the beliefs you developed to stay safe.
- Map the moments that influenced your inner narrative.
- Build the capacity to stay present with early memories.
- Prepare to explore your protective patterns in Pathway Two.

BEFORE YOU BEGIN

Use this section to check your state before starting.
- Make sure you feel steady and present.
- Notice your breath and any tension in your body.
- Keep a grounding practice nearby in case you need it.
- Move slowly and do not push for memories.
- Write only what feels manageable.
- Stop if you feel overwhelmed and return later.

This Pathway works best when you stay curious and follow your natural pace.

KEY CONCEPTS

These ideas guide your work in this Pathway.
- Exile is the separation from parts of you that carried early hurt or unmet needs.
- Adaptations formed to protect you when you lacked support or safety.
- Early roles and personas helped you manage pain or instability.
- Messages from family, culture, and environment shaped your beliefs.
- These early patterns still influence your reactions and relationships.

PATHWAY 1. MAPS OF EXILE

1. STORY

Exile begins quietly. You learn early which parts of you were welcomed and which parts were not. You adjusted to survive. You read the room. You tracked danger. You sensed when to speak and when to stay silent. Over time, you built a version of yourself that kept you safe. That version became familiar, and it became automatic.

Many people carry an Exiled Child inside them. This part holds the first wounds, the early confusion, and the unmet needs that never had room to breathe. The Exiled Child remembers what happened. It remembers the loneliness, the pressure, the fear, or the shame. It remembers the moment you learned to hide a thought, a need, a feeling, or a truth.

This Pathway invites you to trace those early adaptations with clarity. You map the who, what, where, when, and why. You identify the parts and personas that formed. You see how each of them worked to protect the tender child inside you. When you see the map, you begin to reclaim choice.

2. TEACHING

Exile is the separation from parts of yourself that carry pain, fear, shame, or unmet need. These parts were not weak. They were overwhelmed. Other parts stepped in to protect you. Those protective strategies hardened into roles, masks, and learned behaviors.

You work with five elements in this Pathway.

- The origin event. Something happened or failed to happen.
- The adaptive role. You became a version of yourself that the environment could accept.
- The family field. You absorbed rules, expectations, and dynamics.
- The early parts. Each part carried a job, a fear, and a hope.
- The current impact. These patterns continue to influence your life today.

Mapping exile is not about blame. It is about clarity. When you understand what shaped you, you gain freedom to choose new responses.

3. REFLECTION

Use the questions below to map your landscape of exile. Leave space under each prompt for writing.

Origin Map

Consider the earliest moments that shaped your sense of safety or belonging.

- Who was involved. Write their names or roles.

- What happened. Describe the event in simple terms.

- Where it took place. Home, school, outside, or another setting.

- When it began. Approximate age or stage of life.

- Why it mattered. Identify the unmet need.

- What was needed but not received. Be specific.

Message Map

These prompts help you identify messages you absorbed.

- What you learned not to feel. List emotions you pushed away.

- What you learned not to say. Write the words you held back.

- What you learned to do to avoid pain. Name the behaviors.

- What you hid to stay safe. Describe what went underground.

- What role you took on. Clarify the function you filled.

Persona Map

Trace the first adaptive identity you created.

- Which version of you emerged to protect the child. Name it.

- How it acted. Describe the behaviors.

- What it feared. Identify the threat.

- What promises it made. Write the internal vows.

- How it still shows up now. Give examples.

Parts Map

Identify the early parts of you that formed in response to exile.

- Name each part that formed.

- Describe its job. What did it do for you.

- Describe its fear. What was it avoiding.

- Describe its hope. What did it want for you.

- Describe how you feel toward it today. Use one clear sentence.

Impact Map

Look at how these patterns influence your present life.

- How these patterns shape your relationships.

- How they shape your choices.

- How they shape your boundaries.

- How they shape your identity.

- How they shape your sense of safety.

ENTERING PATHWAY 1: BEGINNING THE WORK

Writing Space

RETURN OF THE EXILED CHILD

 ## 4. PRACTICE

These exercises help you build a structured map of your exile. Each exercise includes clearer prompts and designated writing space.

Exercise A. The Exile Timeline

Use this exercise to see the sequence of events that shaped your early adaptations.

Prompts:

- List five to ten moments that shaped your sense of safety, identity, or belonging.

- Write your approximate age.

- Describe what happened.

- Identify who was present.

- Write how you felt in one or two words.

- State what you learned in that moment.

- Write the adaptation or behavior that formed.

Writing Space

Exercise B. The First Persona

Identify the first protective role you created to navigate your environment.

Prompts:

- Write the name of this persona.

- Describe how it acted.

- Identify what it feared.

- State what it protected.

- Write the job it performed for you.

- Describe how it appears today.

Writing Space

Exercise C. The Family Field Scan

This exercise helps you see the rules that shaped your behavior.

Prompts:

- List spoken rules you absorbed.

- List unspoken rules you sensed.

- Describe how each rule shaped your choices.

- Identify which rules still influence you.

Writing Space

Exercise D. Parts Naming

Name the parts that formed in response to exile.

Prompts:

- List each part. One line per part.

- Describe each part's job.

- Identify its fear.

- Identify its hope.

- Write how you feel toward the part today.

Writing Space:

Exercise E. Exile Summary Sheet

Create a one-page summary that captures your map.

Prompts:

- List the key origin events.

- Name the personas that formed.

- List the parts involved.

- Write the rules that shaped you.

- State the adaptations that continue today.

Writing Space:

PATHWAY 1. MAPS OF EXILE

Your life carries moments that landed in your body, shaped your expectations, and influenced how you protect yourself. This timeline helps you identify the key events that formed your patterns. Mark the highs and lows that stand out. Include experiences that shifted your sense of safety, belonging, identity, or responsibility. This tool will support all of the work you do across the five pathways.

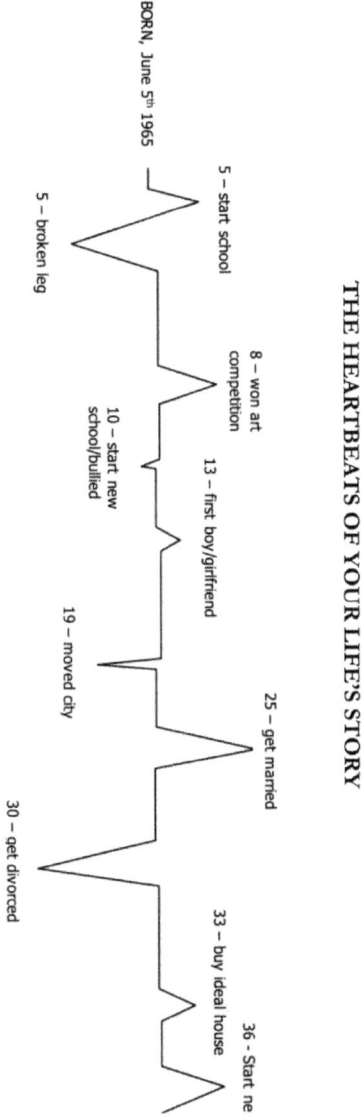

Closing

You have mapped the beginning of your story. You now see where exile formed, how you adapted, and which parts stepped in to protect you. This prepares you for Pathway 2, where you explore the armor, you built to keep the Exiled Child safe.

WALL OF ARMOR

*"What we built to survive becomes the prison we carry.
The armor kept us safe once, but to live, we must lay it down."*
– Keith W. Fiveson

Pathway 2. Wall of Armor

LEARNING OUTCOMES:

- Identify the protective parts that manage your daily life.
- Describe the roles and behaviors these parts use to stay safe.
- Notice how your armor reacts to stress or activation.
- Clarify what each protector is trying to prevent.
- Understand how these strategies helped you adapt.
- Begin separating your present choices from old defenses.
- Prepare to build an internal Sanctuary in Pathway Three.

BEFORE YOU BEGIN

Prepare yourself before examining your protective strategies.
- Notice your current emotional state.
- Identify any part of you that feels guarded.
- Slow your breathing until your body softens.
- Remind yourself that you are safe now.
- Expect discomfort.
- Keep your focus on clarity, not self-judgment.

Move at a speed that keeps you inside your window of tolerance.

KEY CONCEPTS

These ideas help you understand your protective system.
- Armor includes the strategies you use to avoid vulnerability.
- Managers and Protectors act early to prevent discomfort or danger.
- These strategies formed in response to real conditions in your past.
- Armor creates stability but carries emotional and relational costs.
- You can work with armor when you understand what it protects.

PATHWAY 2. WALL OF ARMOR

 1. Story. How the Wall Forms

Many people grow up in environments where emotional or physical safety is not consistent. When this happens, a child adapts quickly to reduce exposure to harm, conflict, or instability. These adaptations become automatic. You learn to read the room, anticipate reactions, and manage other people's moods. You figure out which behaviors prevent anger, chaos, or neglect. You stop expressing certain emotions because they lead to punishment or disapproval. Nothing about this is a conscious choice. It is a survival response.

Over time, these survival behaviors create a wall. You may stay quiet to avoid conflict, stay useful to gain approval, stay angry to protect yourself, or stay numb to avoid overwhelm. These patterns become normal. Eventually, they become who you believe yourself to be.

You build this wall through many micro-moments. You observe adults who cannot regulate themselves and conclude that it is your responsibility to manage the situation. You hide parts of yourself because past experiences showed you that expressing them is unsafe. You develop strategies like control, perfectionism, caretaking, withdrawal, or defensiveness to prevent future harm.

As you age, these strategies mature into recognizable parts, such as the Controller, the Guard, the Performer, the Numb One, the Fixer, or the Judge. Each part believes it must continue its job, even when the original danger no longer exists. These patterns remain because they worked. They kept you functioning. They prevented worse outcomes. They made life manageable.

The purpose of this pathway is to help you understand how this wall functions today, so you can begin to work with it instead of being ruled by it.

Writing Space

2. Teaching. What Armor Does and Why It Stays

Armor is any behavior, attitude, or emotional strategy you use to reduce vulnerability. It helps you keep control, avoid discomfort, or prevent old wounds from being touched. These strategies often form in response to early relational imprints. For example, if you learned that expressing sadness led to criticism, you may have developed a reflex to shut down sadness entirely. If you learned that acting strong earned approval, you may have adopted strength as your primary identity.

These imprints combine with social expectations and cultural conditioning. Many people are taught that certain emotions are weak, that independence is required, or that conflict must be avoided. These ideas reinforce the internal wall because they validate the belief that protection is necessary.

Armor is functional. It helps you perform well at work, stay in control of difficult situations, manage relationships, and maintain a sense of stability. It prevents you from becoming overwhelmed. In many cases, it prevents you from repeating painful experiences from the past.

However, armor also carries significant costs. It interferes with intimacy. It blocks emotional connection. It suppresses vulnerability. It increases internal pressure because managing your own defenses requires constant energy. When you rely on armor for decades, it becomes difficult to distinguish between protection and identity.

The purpose of this pathway is not to remove your armor. It is to understand it. When you understand why your armor formed and what it protects, you gain the ability to choose how you respond instead of relying on automatic patterns.

Writing Space

3. Practice. Working With the Wall

These exercises help you examine your protective strategies in a structured way.

A. Identify Your Protective Strategies

List three strategies you use when you feel stressed, judged, or unsafe. Write one sentence describing how each helps you and one sentence describing how each limits you.

Writing Space

B. Notice What Activates Your Armor

Choose a recent moment when a strategy appeared. Describe the situation and identify the trigger.

Writing Space

C. Explore the Voice of a Protector

Choose one protector. Write a paragraph describing what this part believes it must prevent. Then write another paragraph describing what it wants for you.

Writing Space

D. Evaluate the Cost of a Strategy

List two benefits and two costs of one selected strategy.

Writing Space

E. Ask a Direct Question

Ask one protector, what would you need in order to relax for a moment? Record the response.

Writing Space

4. Reflection. Understanding Your Armor Today

Use full sentences to answer each question.

- How often do your protective strategies appear in daily life?

- Which part feels strongest right now, and why?

- Which behavior feels the oldest or most automatic?

- What situations activate your wall most often?

- What emotions feel unsafe to express?

- What part of your life is still being managed as if the old danger is present?

- What would improve if your armor reduced even slightly?

- What new possibilities would open if your protectors trusted your current capacity?

Writing Space

The Inner Sanctuary

*"Beneath the noise and battle lies a still place.
The sanctuary is not found, it is remembered within breath, within body,
within heart."*

– Keith W. Fiveson

Pathway 3: Inner Sanctuary

LEARNING OUTCOMES:

- Learn how to create a regulated internal space.
- Strengthen your ability to stay present during activation.
- Notice shifts in breath, posture, and sensation.
- Practice meeting protectors from a grounded state.
- Build trust between your Adult Self and your parts.
- Develop reliable tools for returning to center.
- Prepare to examine learned narratives in Pathway Four

BEFORE YOU BEGIN

Settle your system before entering the Sanctuary.
- Sit in a position that supports presence.
- Take three slow breaths with longer exhales.
- Notice your body without changing anything.
- Release expectations or goals for this session.
- Allow quiet to form on its own.

Only continue when your breath feels steady, and you sense enough internal space.

KEY CONCEPTS

These ideas support the development of internal safety.
- Breath regulates your nervous system and widens your awareness.
- The Sanctuary is an internal place of stability and clarity.
- You can meet your parts only when your system feels steady.
- Somatic cues show when your body is open or activated.
- Presence grows when you slow down and release pressure.

Overview

Before you enter this Pathway, pause, and ask yourself a simple question: *What is sanctuary?*

Many people hear that word and think of a church, a sacred room, or a religious space they must earn entry to. But the Sanctuary we explore here is different. It is not built of stone or guided by doctrine. It is not reserved for the worthy or the devout. It does not belong to an institution.

This Sanctuary belongs to you.

It is the inner place where you stop being a collection of roles and reactions and return to being a whole human being. A place where you are not defined by what you have done, what you are doing, or what you will do. A place where the pressure to perform, protect, or prove yourself falls away.

Here, you can remember yourself. Not the fragmented self-made up of parts that work, guard, and manage your survival, but the deeper self that breathes beneath everything. The self that carries the memory of your ancestors, your origins, your essence. The self that knows how to rest and how to be.

This Pathway is a crucible for soul retrieval. A quiet, steady place where the scattered pieces of you can return. A space where your body, mind, spirit, and soul can come back together. You do not need to bring a story with you. In fact, this is the place where story begins to loosen its hold.

When you enter the Inner Sanctuary, you step into the infinite moment, the immortal minute where nothing is required, and everything becomes possible. This is where you begin to live from presence rather than identity. This is where you learn to experience, not interpret. This is where you learn to be, not do.

Tone

This chapter speaks directly to you, guiding you inward with warmth, steadiness, and clarity. The language invites reflection, curiosity, and a softening into your deeper nature. This chapter speaks directly to you. Every section is written to support you, to steady you, and to walk beside you as you explore your inner world.

Core Themes

- You are more than the identity you learned to carry.
- The breath brings you home to yourself.
- Your stories can loosen. You are not defined by them.
- Awareness expands when you slow down.
- You can meet your parts without fear.
- You have a place inside that is untouched by culture or conditioning.
- You can return to that place whenever you choose.

The Inner Sanctuary

There is a place inside you that has never been broken. A place that does not demand anything of you. When you enter the Sanctuary, you step out of the noise and into yourself.

You may notice that your breath softens. You may feel your body become a little heavier, a little more grounded. You may sense a quiet that feels familiar, even if you haven't visited it in years.

This Sanctuary is yours. You do not have to earn access to it. You do not have to deserve it. It has always been here, waiting for you to remember it.

Inside this space, stories lose their power. Identity loosens. The pressure to protect yourself falls away. What remains is a simpler truth: you are here, breathing, aware, present.

Here, you can open the door to deeper layers of yourself without fear that you will be overwhelmed. You can meet your emotions, your memories, and your parts with the same gentle breath that brought you here.

Breath as the Gateway

Your breath is your first doorway into the Sanctuary. When you slow your exhale, your system settles. This softens the grip of your thinking mind and widens your awareness.

You may feel your shoulders drop. You may sense more space between thoughts. You may feel a subtle quiet forming.

This is how the threshold opens. You cross it not by force, but by allowing. Your breath teaches your body that it is safe to soften. Your awareness follows.

Letting Go of the Constructed Self

Throughout your life you absorbed beliefs, expectations, and roles. You learned to become someone the world could understand. You learned to fit into the shape that others needed from you.

None of this was your fault. It was how you survived.

In this Pathway, you do not have to hold any of that. You are invited to recognize that much of what you believe about yourself was formed long before you had any choice.

Here, you can set those beliefs down. You can feel what remains when the pressure to be someone drops away. You can rediscover parts of yourself that were pushed aside or forgotten.

This is the beginning of reclaiming your own nature.

Meeting the Non-Ordinary

As you rest in the Sanctuary, you may notice subtle impressions: a memory fragment, an image, a sensation, a knowing. These are not distractions. They are openings.

This is your inner world rising to meet you. You do not have to interpret anything. You do not have to explain anything. Let the experience be what it is.

Your awareness is widening. Your system is trusting you. You are beginning to feel the layers beneath ordinary consciousness.

Guided Inner Room Practice

This practice helps you enter the Sanctuary with consistency. Move slowly. There is no rush.

Settle

Sit in a position that helps you feel present. Let your feet find the ground. Let your jaw soften. Let the breath come as it is.

Breathe

Let your exhale lengthen. Not forced, just softer. Notice how your body responds.

Turn Inward

Let your attention shift inward. Feel the quiet forming. Do not try to make anything happen. Allow the space to open.

Arrive

You may sense a room-like stillness. You may feel spaciousness or warmth. However, it appears, this is your Sanctuary.

Listen

Let impressions arise naturally. Stay with them gently. You are not here to fix anything. You are here to notice.

Return

When you feel ready, take one slow inhale and a longer exhale. Feel your body again. Let your awareness widen outward.

Writing Space: These pages are for you. Write what you felt. What surprised you. What softened. What shifted. Anything is welcome.

Boundary Mapping Exercise

This exercise helps you understand the forces that shaped your sense of self. It offers clarity without judgment.

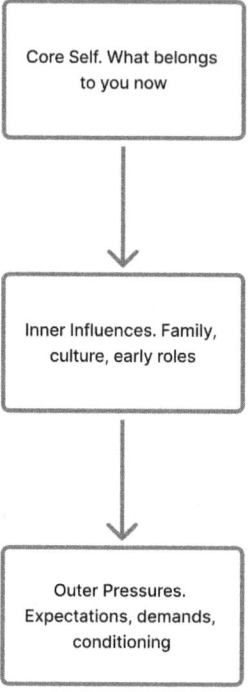

Explore

Think about what shaped you: caregivers, culture, relationships, survival patterns. Notice what you took in.

Name

Write down the roles, beliefs, and expectations that formed within you.

Notice

How do these beliefs show up now? Where do they limit you? Where do they help you?

Choose

Decide what is yours to keep, and what you can begin to release.

Writing Space:

Part Dialogue Template

This is a conversation between you and a part of you that learned to protect you. You meet the part gently, from the Sanctuary.

Identify

Who is here? What does this part feel like? How does it show up?

Understand

Ask the part when it learned its role. What was happening then? What did it need?

Listen

Let the part speak. Let it tell you how it protects you.

Respond

From the Sanctuary, respond with clarity and kindness.

Integrate

Notice any softening. Any shift. Any release.

RETURN OF THE EXILED CHILD

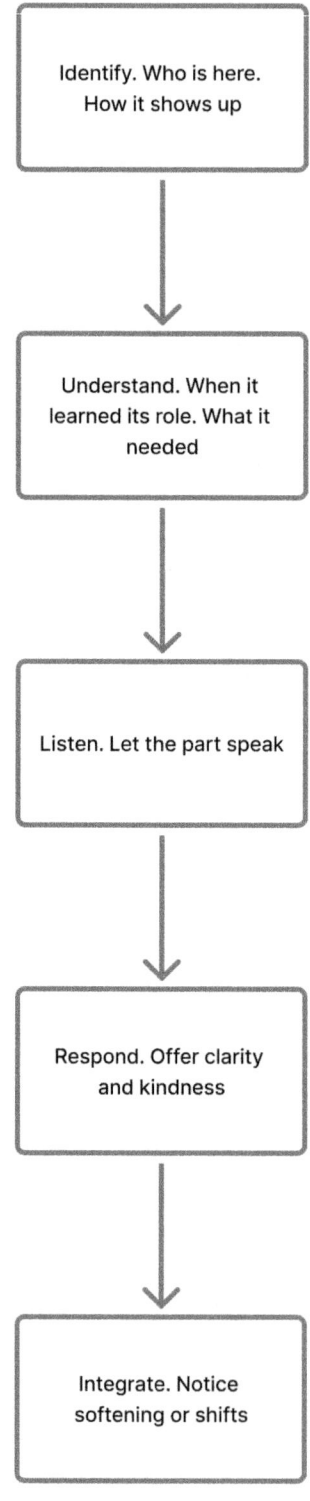

Nervous System Tracking Sheet

Awareness grows when you can see your own patterns.

Track

Each day, notice:

- When you feel activated.
- When you feel contracted.
- When you feel open.
- When you feel expansive.

Observe

Notice what helps you return to yourself. Notice what pulls you away. Notice the shifts.

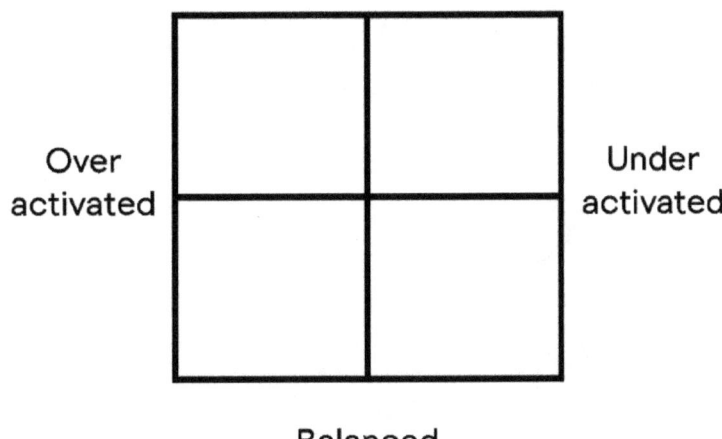

Writing Space: These pages are for you. Write what you felt. What surprised you. What softened. What shifted. Anything is welcome. Weekly chart for morning, afternoon, and evening check-ins.

House of Mirrors

*"In every reflection, a hidden-self calls back.
The mirrors show us what we deny, what we project,
and what we are ready to reclaim."*
— Keith W. Fiveson

Pathway 4. House of Mirrors

LEARNING OUTCOMES:

- Identify the roles you were taught to play.
- Notice beliefs that no longer reflect who you are.
- Clarify distortions formed through pressure or conditioning.
- Explore the impact of inherited narratives.
- Update the stories that shape your identity.
- Strengthen your ability to see yourself accurately.
- Prepare to integrate your system in Pathway Five.

BEFORE YOU BEGIN

Prepare yourself to look at distortion and learned roles.
- Check your level of activation.
- Notice if any protector feels tense or reactive.
- Breathe until your chest or throat softens.
- Remind yourself that you are describing patterns, not judging yourself.
- Commit to honest answers even if they feel awkward.

This Pathway requires directness. Stay grounded as you write.

KEY CONCEPTS

- These ideas help you work with distortion and expression.
- Roles and masks form when honesty feels unsafe.
- Shame distorts your identity and silences your truth.
- Learned behaviors shape how you speak and what you hide.
- Distortion appears when you adjust yourself to protect connection.
- Accurate expression requires clarity, courage, and grounding.

Preparing for Integration

This Pathway gives you the clarity needed to integrate your work. When you complete the House of Mirrors, you understand the beliefs, roles, and internal narratives that shaped your identity. You enter Pathway Five with more accuracy, less confusion, and a grounded sense of who you are now.

Use these exercises whenever old stories surface. Clarity grows each time you question a belief and update your understanding.

Story: How We Learn to Distort Ourselves

Every person learns early how to shape their identity to fit their environment. You adjust your tone, your posture, your mood, and even your truth to preserve connection or avoid conflict. Over time, these adjustments become automatic. You begin to forget where the performance ends and where your real voice begins. This is the House of Mirrors. Here, reflections distort reality, and you learn to survive by bending your truth to protect yourself.

Sometimes you exaggerate strength, so no one sees your hurt. Sometimes you shrink so no one feels threatened. Sometimes you stay silent because the cost of honesty feels too high. Many people carry two versions of themselves. The public self that manages perception. The private self that holds unspoken thoughts, quiet shame, hidden desires, or unprocessed anger. The split can last for decades.

This is not failure. This is adaptation. When you grow up in environments where honesty is punished, where needs are dismissed, or where truth creates chaos, you learn to silence yourself. You learn to protect yourself by becoming who others expect you to be. You begin to believe that your real truth is dangerous, or too much, or not enough.

This Pathway asks you to face these distortions without collapsing into shame or hardening into defense. You explore how your identity formed around other people's expectations. You uncover the masks you wear to keep people close or keep them away. You learn to distinguish your real voice from the conditioned voice learned long ago.

Writing Space: What parts of your identity feel shaped by survival rather than authenticity?

2. Teaching. Understanding Expression, Avoidance, and Self-Disclosure

Truth becomes distorted when safety is uncertain. You learn to hide feelings that caused conflict. You learn to speak in ways that stabilize the environment. You learn to stay silent when your needs interfere with someone else's comfort. These habits form a protective system that keeps you secure but cuts you off from your authentic voice.

Many people develop roles to navigate life. You may become the Performer who tries to impress others. You may become the Peacemaker who avoids tension. You may become the Prosecutor who attacks first to avoid being exposed. You may become the Chameleon who blends into every environment. These identities keep you functional but prevent you from being fully known.

Shame reinforces these roles. Shame tells you that your truth is unacceptable. Shame tells you that your needs are inconvenient. Shame convinces you that silence is safer than honesty. When shame is left unaddressed, the mask becomes the identity.

Expression becomes healing when it becomes accurate. You learn to name what you feel without apology. You learn to set boundaries without fear. You learn to speak without managing the reactions of others. This is how integrity is restored. This is how real connection is formed. This is how your voice becomes a source of strength rather than a risk.

Writing Space: Which roles or masks do you recognize in yourself? Where did you learn them?

Pathway Four helps you see the patterns, beliefs, and learned stories that shaped how you understand yourself. This section focuses on clarity. You identify the influences that formed your identity, the roles you adopted to stay safe, and the distorted reflections you absorbed from family, culture, and lived experience. You learn to recognize what is yours and what was inherited or imposed.

House of Mirrors work is direct and practical. You examine the beliefs that guide your behavior, the narratives that shape your decisions, and the internal voices that influence your emotions. This is not about blame. It is about understanding the systems that shaped you so you can make informed choices about what you carry forward.

Pathway Four gives you structured exercises to map your beliefs, question distortions, and update narratives that no longer support your well-being. Each exercise helps you separate past conditioning from your present experience. The goal is to see yourself accurately and to act from clarity rather than old patterns.

Seeing Your Reflections Clearly

You learned who you were through the responses and reactions of others. Some reflections were accurate. Others were distorted by their fears, expectations, and unresolved histories. These reflections shaped how you saw yourself.

Reflection Exercise

1. Write down the roles you were expected to play.

Include family roles, school roles, social roles, and any identity that was assigned to you.

2. Identify where each role came from.

Name the person, environment, or message that taught you this role.

3. Ask if the role reflects who you are now.

Be direct. Keep your answers simple.

4. Circle the roles you no longer want to carry.

Writing Space:

Identifying Distortions

Distortions are beliefs that formed under pressure. They usually begin with someone else's fear, shame, or limitation. When repeated often enough, they become internal truths.

Distortion Mapping

1. Write down a belief you learned about yourself.

Examples include "I am too much," "I am not enough," or "I have to keep the peace."

2. Describe where the belief came from.

Be specific.

3. Note how this belief shaped your behavior.

Describe the actions you took to match or avoid this belief.

4. Decide if the belief is accurate today.

Answer with clarity.

Updating Your Story

When you see distortions clearly, you can rewrite the narrative. This is not about erasing your past. It is about creating an honest and grounded understanding of who you are now.

Narrative Update

1. Choose one distortion or outdated story.

Write it down plainly.

2. Write a corrected version based on your present self.

Keep this short and direct.

3. List the behaviors that support the updated story.

4. Identify the situations where you tend to slip into the old pattern.

Write how you will return to clarity.

PATHWAY 4. HOUSE OF MIRRORS

Writing Space:

3. REFLECTION. Questions That Cut Through Illusion

Use these questions slowly.
Answer without defensiveness.
Let your voice tell the truth.

- When did you first learn that honesty had consequences?

- Who taught you to shrink so others felt more comfortable?

- What emotions do you hide because you fear judgment?

- What part of you becomes louder when you feel insecure?

- What truth do you avoid because saying it might change a relationship?

- What mask helps you feel accepted but leaves you exhausted?

PATHWAY 4. HOUSE OF MIRRORS

- What role did you play in your family that you still play now?

- What do you reveal to others, and what do you conceal?

- What anger hides a deeper vulnerability you were never allowed to show?

- What desire have you never said out loud because you fear rejection?

Prompts for Your Blank Journey Map

Writing Space: Answer the questions that stand out to you.

Writing Space:

4. Practice. Reclaiming Voice and Integrity

Exercise 1. Mirror Statement Practice

Write a sentence starting with "I have been pretending that…"

Complete ten versions.

This shows you where you perform instead of express.

Writing Space:

Exercise 2. Boundary Rehearsal

Write three direct boundaries you want to express.

Read them aloud.

Notice where your body tightens or hesitates.

Writing Space:

Exercise 3. Shame Exposure Exercise

Choose one memory you keep hidden.

Describe it factually.

Write what you feared.

Write what you needed.

This reframes shame into compassion.

Writing Space:

Exercise 4. Voice Tracking Practice

Track each moment you hesitate before speaking.
Document what you wanted to say, what you said instead, and what you feared.

Writing Space:

Exercise 5. Truth Calibration Exercise

Identify one small truth you can safely express this week.

Speak it to someone you trust.

Start with something manageable.

Writing Space:

Closing: Completing Pathway Four

You have taken an honest look at the beliefs, roles, and learned stories that shaped how you see yourself. This work is challenging, and it requires clarity. By identifying distortions and naming the influences that shaped your self-image, you create the conditions for real change. You begin to separate who you are from what you absorbed.

As you finish this Pathway, notice what feels more accurate now. Notice the beliefs that no longer fit and the roles you are ready to release. You are not erasing your past. You are understanding it in a new way. This clarity prepares you for the next stage of the work.

Pathway Five builds on everything you discovered here. With a clearer sense of self, you are ready to integrate your parts, strengthen your internal leadership, and move toward a grounded sense of wholeness. Move forward at your own pace. Stay connected to your breath. Let each insight settle before you continue.

Journey Home

*"The journey home is not a return to what was lost,
it is a union with what was never truly gone."*
— Keith W. Fiveson

Pathway 5. The Journey Home: Integration

> **LEARNING OUTCOMES:**
>
> - Identify the parts that need your steady leadership.
> - Strengthen your connection with your Exiled Child.
> - Clarify what integration means for your system.
> - Practice leading with clarity, calm, and intention.
> - Align daily behaviors with your updated story.
> - Build internal agreements that support long-term change.
> - Prepare for ongoing integration in the final chapter.

> **BEFORE YOU BEGIN**
>
> Take a moment to orient before starting integration work.
> - Notice how you feel after completing the earlier Pathways.
> - Identify which part is most active right now.
> - Slow your breathing until your focus stabilizes.
> - Release pressure to be perfect or complete.
> - Bring your attention to your adult self.
>
> **You are stepping into integration. Move with intention and steadiness.**

> **KEY CONCEPTS**
>
> These ideas guide your integration work.
> - Integration means bringing all parts into relationship with your adult self.
> - Imprints are old patterns that can be named and updated.
> - Character energies become resources when they cooperate.
> - Sanctuary practices help you respond with intention in daily life.
> - You strengthen leadership when you act from your adult self.

Pathway 5. The Journey Home: Integration

Integration brings together the work you completed in the five Pathways. It helps you understand how your system has changed and what you need to stay grounded as you move forward. This chapter focuses on daily practices that strengthen regulation, support clarity, and reinforce new patterns.

You learned a great deal about your internal world. You identified early imprints, protective responses, roles, and distorted beliefs. You connected with parts that shaped your behaviors and emotions. Integration helps you hold these insights with steadiness. It turns understanding into action.

Integration is practical. It relies on simple behaviors that help your nervous system stay regulated. It highlights the tools you return to when you feel activated or overwhelmed. It supports you in building consistency, even when old patterns surface.

The goal of integration is not perfection. The goal is awareness, choice, and stability. As you use these practices, you strengthen your capacity to respond instead of reacting. You learn to support your system with clarity. You build a foundation you can rely on.

Move through this chapter at your own pace. Practice the skills that feel most supportive. Return to any tool whenever you need it. Integration is ongoing. Each day gives you another chance to reinforce what you have learned.

1. Story. Returning to Yourself

The Journey Home brings together everything explored in the previous pathways. This is where you begin living with your parts rather than fighting them or letting them operate without your awareness. You return to your core identity by understanding why these parts formed and how they helped you survive. Throughout your life, each strategy you developed shaped an internal character. The Exiled Child carries early hurt and unmet needs. The Protector shields you from further harm. The Strategist anticipates danger and creates plans. The Caregiver attends to others to maintain stability. The Witness tracks shifts in tone, mood, and behavior.

In this pathway, these parts come into conscious relationship. You learn how to sit at the same internal table with them, hear what each carries, and respond from your adult self with clarity rather than fear. This is where the sanctuary you have built internally becomes something you can take into the world. You begin responding with intention rather than reacting from habit. You bring honesty into conversations, steadiness into challenges, and grounded awareness into relationships.

The Journey Home marks the shift from internal exploration to embodied practice. It emphasizes consistency, honesty, and the willingness to show up for yourself with the same care and attention you may have given others for years.

Writing Space:

2. Teaching. Living From the Integrated Self

Integration means bringing all of your internal parts into a coherent relationship under the leadership of your adult self. It does not erase history or complexity. It allows you to recognize why your parts formed, update them with the reality of your present life, and create more choice in how you respond. When integration strengthens, you feel more grounded and less fragmented. You understand what you feel, why you feel it, and how to act in alignment with your values.

A central element of integration is recognizing imprints. These are patterns formed through family, culture, trauma, and conditioning. Until named, they operate automatically. When you identify an imprint and understand which part carries it, you gain the ability to revise it and offer your parts more accurate information.

You also work with the different character energies you developed. Each one holds a distinct strength or perspective. The Child holds vulnerability and truth. The Protector holds boundaries. The Strategist holds structure and planning. The Caregiver holds empathy. The Witness holds awareness. These energies become resources once they learn to cooperate.

Bringing the sanctuary into the external world means applying this understanding in daily life. You pause before reacting, check in with your parts, and choose aligned action. You bring clarity into conflict, steadiness into uncertainty, and presence into relationships. This is the practical expression of living an integrated life.

Writing Space:

3. Practice. Embodying the Journey Home

Practice 1. The Inner Table Exercise

Identify the part most active today and the emotion or belief it carries. Name what the part wants or fears, then respond from your adult self with reassurance or updated information. This builds trust and reduces automatic reactions.

Writing Space:

Practice 2. Imprint Mapping

Name one imprint that influences your behavior. Identify its earliest memory and how it shaped your choices. Name the part that carries it and offer updated information. Define the new pattern you want to practice.

Writing Space:

Practice 3. Carrying the Sanctuary into Daily Life

Choose a situation where you tend to lose your center. Identify which part takes over and describe how your adult self will intervene. Write a clear intention and include your plan for repair if needed.

Writing Space:

Practice 4. Integration Breath Check

Use a simple breathing rhythm: inhale for 4, hold for 2, exhale for 6. Ask which part is present and what it needs, then respond from your adult self.

Writing Space:

4. Reflection. Who Are You Becoming?

Reflect on the changes you have experienced, the parts that have softened, and the values that guide you now. Explore how relationships feel different, what patterns you want to release, and what it means to live with self-leadership.

Writing Space:

INTEGRATION AND SKILL BUILDING:

> **LEARNING OUTCOMES:**
> - Understand what integration looks like in daily life.
> - Use practical skills to regulate your system.
> - Strengthen patterns that support stability.
> - Notice early signs of activation and respond with choice.
> - Reinforce the updated narratives you created.
> - Build consistency through simple daily practices.
> - Prepare to carry this work forward over time.

Practices You Can Use Every Day

This chapter gives you tools you can rely on after you complete the five Pathways. These practices help you notice activation early, regulate your system, repair ruptures, and return to your adult self with clarity. The tools are simple, repeatable, and effective. You can use them in any situation where you feel overwhelmed, disconnected, or uncertain.

Integration happens through practice. It is not a single insight. It is a daily process of returning to yourself.

1. Noticing Activation

Activation is the first signal that a part of you has stepped forward. You cannot prevent activation, but you can learn to recognize it quickly and respond in a grounded way.

Practice: Early Detection Scan

Use this scan once in the morning, once in the evening, and any time you feel a shift.

Scan these areas carefully:
- Chest pressure
- Throat tightness
- Stomach tension
- Shallow breath
- Heat or cold
- Restlessness
- Sudden withdrawal

- Urge to fix, manage, or argue
- Narrative escalation ("I must, I should, I can't")

Write what you notice without analysis.
This builds awareness and prevents escalation.

Writing Space:

2. Stopping Escalation

After activation begins, you have a short window where you can stop escalation and shift your state.

Practice: Thirty-Second Reset

Use this whenever you feel yourself tightening or slipping into old patterns.

Step 1. Exhale longer than you inhale

Count four in, six out.

Step 2. Drop your shoulders

This interrupts tension patterns.

Step 3. Soften your jaw and tongue

This signals your nervous system to slow down.

Step 4. Say quietly to yourself:

"I notice what is happening."

This resets your system enough to make a clear choice.

3. Returning to Your Adult Self

Your adult self leads the system. When protectors take over, you need a reliable method to return to the part of you that can choose, speak clearly, and act with intention.

Practice: The Three Questions

Ask these questions in order.
Do not skip steps.

1. **Who is here?**
   Name the part that stepped forward.

2. **What does this part want to prevent?**
   Identify the fear or threat it perceives.

3. **What does my adult self-want to do right now?**
   State a clear, intentional action.

This short sequence restores leadership of your internal system.

4. Managing Overwhelm

Overwhelm happens when activation exceeds your capacity. These tools help you reduce internal pressure and create space so you can think more clearly.

Practice: Grounding Through Contact

Use this when emotions feel loud, fast, or unmanageable.

- Sit down if possible.
- Place one hand on your chest.
- Place the other on your abdomen.
- Slow your exhale.
- Feel the weight of your body on the chair or the floor.
- Notice five sounds in the room.

You are teaching your body that you are here and safe.

5. Repairing Ruptures

Ruptures happen in all relationships. Repair is a skill that strengthens connection instead of damaging it. Repair requires honesty, clarity, and presence. It does not require perfection.

Practice: The Repair Sequence

Use this after conflict or misalignment.

Step 1. Return to center

Use any regulation tool above.

Step 2. State your part in the rupture

"I reacted quickly."

"I shut down."

"I made an assumption."

Step 3. Clarify your intention

"I want to understand."

"I want to stay connected."

"I want to communicate clearly."

Step 4. State one concrete need

"I need time."

"I need clarity."

"I need honesty."

This prevents defensiveness and supports reconnection.

6. Planning for Difficult Moments

Difficult moments will happen. Planning gives you stability and reduces confusion.

Practice: The Activation Plan

Write your answers:

- What situations activate you most often.

- What parts usually show up.

- What physical cues appear first.

- What skill you will use first.

- Who you can contact if you need support.

Keep this plan where you can see it. Use it before entering predictable stress.

7. Micro-Sanctuary for Daily Life

Sanctuary is not only a room inside you. It is a practice you carry throughout your day. These small moments prevent overwhelm and restore clarity.

Practice: Micro-Sanctuary Check-Ins

Use these at three points in the day: morning, midday, evening.

1. One slow inhale
2. One long exhale
3. Notice one sensation
4. Notice one emotion
5. Notice one part present
6. Ask: "What do I need right now?"

This keeps you connected to yourself even in busy or stressful environments.

8. Practicing New Behaviors

Change happens through repetition. This practice helps you strengthen new behaviors and weaken old patterns.

Practice: Daily Behavior Anchor

Choose one behavior you want to build this week.

Examples:

- pausing before responding
- speaking one truth each day
- asking for clarity instead of assuming
- setting one boundary
- resting instead of pushing

At the end of each day, answer:

- Did I practice this behavior today
- What helped me
- What made it difficult
- What I will do tomorrow

This keeps the work active.

9. Integration Reflection: Who You Are Becoming

Write in complete thoughts.

Answer these questions clearly.

- What you understand about yourself now

- What changed in your internal system

- How your boundaries shifted

- How your voice changed

- How you relate to your parts differently

- What you want to continue practicing

- How you want to show up in your life now

This reflection completes the cycle of the Workbook and strengthens the integration process.

Writing Space:

Completing the Journey Home

What brought you here. When you began, were you aware of how often you left yourself to stay safe, to belong, or to be needed. Did you notice the moments where adaptation quietly became habit. The first steps asked you to look without judgment at where exile began, and to recognize that what once protected you also carried a cost.

As you moved forward, what did you discover about the armor you built. Could you see how strength, control, pleasing, or withdrawal served a purpose. Did you begin to sense that these strategies were not flaws, but intelligent responses shaped by earlier experiences. And once named, did they start to loosen their grip.

When you learned to return to the body and the breath, what shifted. Did presence become something you practiced rather than something you hoped for. Were there moments when regulation replaced reaction, even briefly. Did you experience how steadiness creates choice.

As you explored the stories you carry, did you notice which ones felt inherited, rehearsed, or incomplete. Could you hear your own voice more clearly beneath them. And when you reached the Journey Home, did you sense that integration is less about fixing and more about relating differently to what is already here.

What you have done is not to arrive at an ending, but to develop a capacity. A capacity to notice when you drift. A capacity to pause. A capacity to return with awareness rather than force. How might this show up in your daily life, in moments of stress, in connection, in rest?

Before continuing, what do you notice now. In your body. In your breath. In your sense of orientation. What feels more available than when you began?

The section that follows is an Appendix. It is not required for your personal journey. It is offered for those who wish to hold this work for others, or to return to it in a guiding role. What choice feels right for you at this moment?

Either way, the work continues where life meets you. And the question is no longer whether you will lose your way, but how gently and how often you can return.

Appendix A:
Facilitator Guide

This guide supports anyone facilitating this Workbook with individuals or groups. It outlines pacing, safety, and session structure. It is not clinical instruction. It provides practical guidance to ensure that the Workbook is used in a grounded, trauma-sensitive way.

1. Purpose of This Guide

This guide provides a clear structure for using the Workbook in one-on-one sessions or small groups. It explains how to support participants as they move through the five Pathways. It highlights safety considerations, pacing, containment strategies, and practical ways to introduce the material.

The goal is to create a grounded, stable environment where individuals can explore their inner system with clarity and steadiness.

2. Preparing to Facilitate

Effective facilitation begins with preparation. Review the Workbook before leading others. Understand the sequence of the five Pathways and the intention behind each one. Make sure the environment is quiet and free of interruptions. Start each session with a brief grounding or breathing practice. This helps participants settle into the work.

Encourage participants to move at a pace that supports nervous system stability. Emphasize that the work is not a race and does not need to be completed on a schedule.

3. Principles of Trauma-Sensitive Facilitation

Trauma-sensitive facilitation requires clarity, presence, and awareness of safety. Use these principles during all sessions:

- Support the participant's pace instead of directing the process.
- Prioritize regulation before insight.
- Avoid pushing for memories or emotional intensity.
- Redirect attention to breath, posture, and sensory awareness when needed.
- Acknowledge protective responses with respect rather than confrontation.
- Treat all emotional states as valid and workable.

These principles create a stable foundation for exploration.

4. Signs of Activation to Watch For

Facilitators should monitor subtle shifts that signal overwhelm or activation. Common indicators include:

- shallow breathing
- tightening in the chest or throat
- rapid speech
- sudden silence
- fidgeting or restlessness
- gaze aversion
- emotional flooding
- collapse in posture
- mental confusion or disorientation

If you observe any of these cues, pause the exercise and guide the participant back into grounding and breath.

5. When to Pause or Stop an Exercise

A session should pause or stop when:

- the participant becomes overwhelmed
- a protector part takes over
- the participant cannot remain in the present moment
- dissociation begins
- breath becomes shallow or irregular
- emotional intensity exceeds their capacity

Focus on restoring regulation. It is better to stop an exercise early than push through a difficult moment. Reinforce that stopping is a healthy response, not a setback.

6. A Simple Session Model

Use this structure for a 60- or 90-minute session:

1. **Opening Grounding (3 to 5 minutes)**
   Use breath, posture, and sensory awareness.

2. **Check-In (5 minutes)**
   Ask what is present in their body, breath, and emotional state.

3. **Workbook Exploration (30 to 50 minutes)**
   Choose one section or exercise. Move slowly. Ask open questions.

4. **Reflection (10 minutes)**
   Invite the participant to name one insight, one part that appeared, and one thing they want to practice.

5. **Closing Grounding (3 to 5 minutes)**
   Use breath or a simple body scan to settle the system.

End the session with clear boundaries. Do not leave a participant in an activated state.

7. Facilitating the Five Pathways

Each Pathway has different energetic and emotional requirements. These notes help you support the participant safely.

Pathway 1: Maps of Exile

Focus on clarity and gentle curiosity. Participants may uncover early messages, unmet needs, or painful memories. Keep the pace slow and emphasize regulation.

Pathway 2: Wall of Armor

Protectors may appear strongly here. Validate them. Do not challenge them. Ask how these strategies helped the participant survive. Respect their purpose.

Pathway 3: Inner Sanctuary

This Pathway supports regulation and presence. Reinforce grounding skills. Encourage slow breathwork and body awareness. This is the safest stage for deeper inquiry.

Pathway 4: House of Mirrors

Shame, distortion, or confusion may surface. Maintain a steady tone and remind the participant that learned roles are not identity. Support clarity without pressure.

Pathway 5: Journey Home

Integration becomes the focus. Encourage the participant to notice shifts, updated boundaries, and internal leadership. Celebrate progress without idealizing perfection.

8. Supporting Group Work

If you use the Workbook in a group, establish the following agreements:

- confidentiality
- respectful listening
- no fixing or advising
- equal speaking time
- permission to pass
- grounding as needed
- a structured closing ritual

Use short dyads or triads for reflection. Keep the group size small enough to maintain safety.

9. Red Flags and When to Refer

Some situations require clinical support. Refer out when you observe:

- persistent emotional flooding
- dissociation that does not resolve with grounding
- disclosure of active self-harm
- signs of untreated trauma that exceed your scope
- severe anxiety or panic
- substance-related instability
- delusional thinking or loss of reality contact

A referral is an act of care, not rejection.

10. Aftercare and Integration

Encourage participants to take ten minutes after every session to settle. Suggest simple practices:

- drink water
- take a slow walk
- write a brief reflection
- sit quietly in a calm environment

Remind them that integration continues between sessions. Encourage them to revisit breathwork, grounding, and the Integration Chapter consistently.

Appendix B: Mini Glossary

This glossary defines important terms used throughout the Workbook. Each definition is written in simple language to support clarity. Use this section whenever you want to review a word or deepen your understanding of the inner system.

Activation
A shift in your nervous system that signals a part has stepped forward. Activation can appear as tension, pressure, heat, withdrawal, or racing thoughts.

Activation Plan
A written plan that prepares you for difficult moments by identifying your triggers, early cues, and the first tool you will use to regulate.

Adult Self
The part of you that observes, regulates, and responds with clarity. The Adult Self leads your internal system.

Awareness
The ability to notice thoughts, sensations, and emotional shifts without merging with them. Awareness creates space for choice.

Boundary
A clear limit that protects your time, energy, body, or emotional space. Boundaries come from clarity.

Breath Regulation
A practice that shifts your nervous system by slowing your exhale, softening your jaw, relaxing your shoulders, and bringing steadiness to your breath.

Collapse
A state where the system withdraws or shuts down because it feels overwhelmed. Collapse may appear as numbness, quietness, or mental fog.

Contact Points
Grounding practices that involve placing a hand on the chest or abdomen to calm the nervous system.

Distortion
A learned pattern or belief formed under stress or shame. Distortion affects how you see yourself and how you act to stay safe.

Exile
A part of you that holds early hurt, unmet needs, or emotional burdens that were too overwhelming at the time.

Firefighter
A protector that reacts quickly to stop emotional pain. Firefighters rely on intense behaviors to create distance from discomfort.

Grounding
A practice that brings attention back to the present moment through breath, posture, or sensory focus.

House of Mirrors
Pathway 4 of the Workbook. This Pathway examines roles, masks, and distortions that shaped your identity.

Identify
The first step in part dialogue. This is the moment you recognize which part is present and how it shows up.

Imprint
A learned pattern, belief, or emotional expectation formed through repeated experiences. Imprints shape automatic reactions.

Inner Child
A younger part of you that carries memories, emotions, and needs from earlier periods in your life.

Inner Sanctuary
Pathway 3 of the Workbook. This is the internal space where you regulate, breathe, and meet your parts with steadiness.

Integration
The process of bringing parts of you into relationship with your Adult Self. Integration increases clarity and coherence.

Journey Home
Pathway 5 of the Workbook. This Pathway supports integration and intentional leadership of your inner system.

Manager
A protector that works in advance to prevent discomfort by controlling situations, emotions, or behaviors.

Mask
A behavior or role used to protect vulnerability or gain acceptance.

Micro-Sanctuary
A brief regulation practice that reconnects you to your center using a few slow breaths.

Orphan
A deeper Exile that feels alone, forgotten, or unprotected. The Orphan often carries early wounds that shaped long-term patterns.

Part
An aspect of your internal system with its own feelings, history, and role.

Part Dialogue
A structured conversation with a part that helps you understand its role, fears, and needs while responding from your Adult Self.

Pattern
A repeated emotional or behavioral response shaped by experience or imprint.

Persona
A role or identity created to function in certain environments.

APPENDIX C: BLANK TOOLS AND MAPS

Presence
A state of steady awareness where you observe your experience without overwhelm.

Protector
A part that keeps you safe by managing emotions, preventing risk, or distancing you from pain.

Regulation
The ability to bring your nervous system back into balance through breath, grounding, and awareness.

Repair
A process of restoring connection after conflict or misalignment through clarity and intention.

Rupture
A break in connection during conflict or misunderstanding.

Sanctuary
An internal space entered through breath and intention that supports regulation and safety.

Self
Your core center that holds clarity, compassion, curiosity, and leadership.

Shutdown
A protective state where the system becomes still or numb.

Somatic Cue
A physical signal that reveals your internal state.

Trigger
An event or stimulus that activates a part or imprint.

Wall of Armor
Pathway 2 of the Workbook. This Pathway explores the defenses and strategies you developed to stay safe.

Window of Tolerance
The range where your nervous system can feel, think, and process without overwhelm or shutdown.

Appendix C:
Blank Tools and Maps

This section contains blank versions of the key diagrams, worksheets, and maps used throughout the Workbook. These tools support ongoing practice, self-reflection, and integration. Print them, copy them, or revisit them whenever you want to deepen your work.

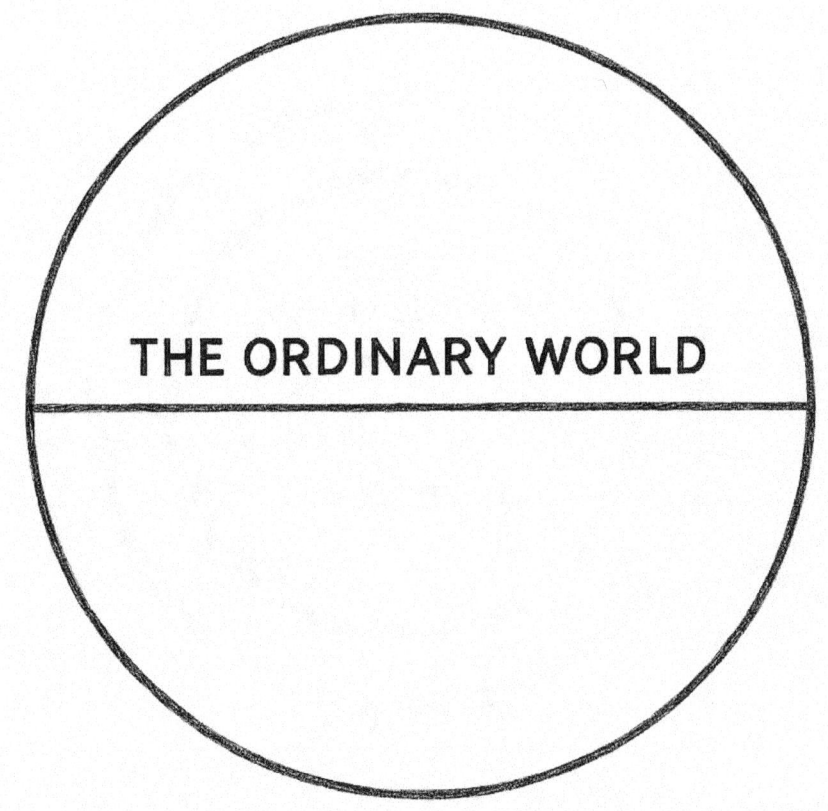

BLANK BOUNDARY MAP

A three ring map of
Self, Inner Influences and
Outer Pressures

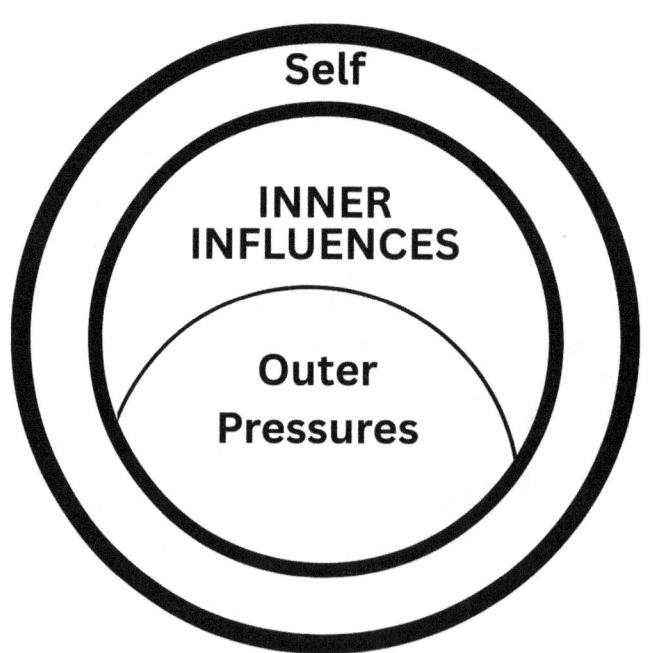

BLANK PERSONA MAP

Use this simple template to idenfiy the various roles, masks, and adaptive identities

Roles

Masks

Adaptive Identities

EXILE SUMMARY SHEET

Use this page to identify unmet needs and early imprints

UNMET NEEDS

EARLY IMPRINTS

Your Story Now

Who You Are Now?

1. What do you understand about yourself that you did not see before?

2. What shifted in your internal system?

3. What did you learn about your Exiled Child?

4. How has your relationship with your protectors changed?

5. What boundaries became clearer to you?

6. What truth do you feel ready to express more openly?

How You Want to Live Now?

1. What do you want to practice in your daily life?

2. How will you return to center when you become activated?

3. What commitments are you ready to make to your Adult Self?

4. What commitments are you ready to make to your Exiled Child?

5. What support do you need as you continue your work?

6. What story are you writing now?

Letter to My Future Self

Use this page to speak directly to the person you are becoming. Write in complete thoughts. Be honest, specific, and grounded.

Dear Future, Me,

Further Reading and Resources

These resources support deeper study and continued reflection.

Inner Parts and Archetypes

- Richard C. Schwartz, *Internal Family Systems Therapy*
- Carl Jung, *The Archetypes, and the Collective Unconscious*
- James Hollis, *Living Between Worlds*

Trauma and Somatic Awareness

- Bessel van der Kolk, *The Body Keeps the Score*
- Peter Levine, *Waking the Tiger*
- Pat Ogden, *Trauma, and the Body*

Myth and Narrative

- Joseph Campbell, *The Hero with a Thousand Faces*
- Maureen Murdock, *The Heroine's Journey*
- Michael Meade, *Fate, and Destiny*

Mindfulness and Presence

- Jon Kabat-Zinn, *Wherever You Go, There You Are*
- Pema Chödrön, *When Things Fall Apart*
- Thich Nhat Hanh, *The Miracle of Mindfulness*

These works expand the ideas, traditions, and practices that inform this workbook. They offer pathways for continued growth, understanding, and integration.

Acknowledgements

This workbook grew from lived experience, sustained practice, and the generosity of many teachers, clinicians, and communities whose work has shaped my understanding of healing and human development. I am grateful for the lineages, traditions, and contemporary clinical frameworks that informed this material and helped create a system that weaves together Internal Family Systems, archetypal psychology, contemplative practice, and the narrative arc of the Hero's Journey.

I extend deep appreciation to Dr. Richard C. Schwartz, founder of Internal Family Systems, whose pioneering work created the foundation for understanding parts and the inherent wisdom of the Self. His model continues to guide my personal and professional journey, and his contributions appear here with gratitude and attribution. I also acknowledge the IFS Institute for its dedication to training, education, and compassionate clinical practice.

I want to honor Dr. Stanislav Grof, whose groundbreaking work in transpersonal psychology and the study of holotropic states broadened our understanding of consciousness, trauma, and the pathways to healing. His insights helped open the door to deeper inquiry into the psyche and the transformative potential of expanded states of awareness.

My gratitude extends to Joseph Campbell, whose articulation of the Hero's Journey provided a universal template for understanding transformation and the psychological forces that arise along the path. His work offered a narrative structure that supports the exploration of inner experience through myth, meaning, and symbolic integration.

I wish to acknowledge Dr. Gabor Maté, whose compassionate and incisive work on trauma, addiction, and the mind-body connection has profoundly influenced the way I understand suffering, resilience, and the conditions necessary for healing. His teachings helped shape the trauma-informed foundation upon which this Workbook rests.

I also want to thank Jon Kabat-Zinn, whose contributions to mindfulness, stress reduction, and somatic awareness helped bring contemplative practice into modern clinical settings. His approach informed the mindful tone of this Workbook and supported the integration of awareness, presence, and compassionate inquiry into this process.

I am grateful for Dr. Miles Neale and the Nalanda Institute for Contemplative Science, whose teachings wove Buddhist psychology, compassion training, and contemplative depth into my work. Their scholarship and guidance helped shape the compassionate lens through which you are invited to meet your inner parts.

My appreciation extends to the Integrative Psychiatry Institute, whose curriculum and faculty deepened my understanding of trauma, integrative care, and evidence-based approaches to mental health. Their teachings supported the blending of clinical insight with practical tools that appear throughout this Workbook.

I also acknowledge MAPS for its decades of research into trauma, consciousness, and the therapeutic potential of expanded states. Their leadership and scientific rigor influenced the broader context in which this work developed and continues to evolve.

I remain grateful to the many mentors, colleagues, and communities acknowledged in my earlier book, *The Mindfulness Experience*, whose influence continues to shape my vision and practice. Your support, teachings, and example helped form the foundation upon which this project was built.

I offer sincere thanks to those who shared their stories, experiences, and vulnerabilities with me over the years. Your trust helped refine the exercises, reflections, and language contained here. Your courage and honesty shaped this Workbook in essential ways.

I also wish to thank the editors, designers, artists, and collaborators whose commitment, patience, and attention strengthened every aspect of this project. Your contributions helped bring this Workbook into a clear and grounded form.

Finally, I want to acknowledge you, the reader and participant. Your willingness to explore your inner world gives purpose to this work. Your courage to meet your history, your parts, and your internal landscape with clarity and compassion brings meaning to these pages. I am grateful for the opportunity to accompany you on this journey.

Closing Reflection

You have reached the end of this Workbook, and before anything else, I want to acknowledge the courage it took for you to get here. You walked through memories, imprints, protectors, and the parts of yourself that once felt too painful or too distant to touch. You practiced slowing down, listening inward, and meeting your system with honesty. None of that is easy, and none of it should be taken lightly.

As you close these pages, take a quiet moment, and check in with yourself. Notice what feels different, even if the difference is small. Notice what softened, what opened, or what simply became more familiar. Notice the parts that surprised you, and the ones that still feel guarded or unsure. There is no expectation for completion. You do not have to resolve everything. You only need to recognize that you showed up for yourself.

I want to share something personally. I did not create this Workbook from a place of mastery or distance. I created it from inside the work itself. I have sat with my own Exiles, met my own Protectors, and listened to the stories I carried for decades. I learned from my mistakes, my defenses, my numbing, and my longing for clarity. I am still learning. I am still growing. I am still meeting parts of myself that have waited years to be heard. This process continues to teach me, and I expect it always will.

If you feel unfinished, or if questions remain, or if parts of you still ache for attention, you are not failing. You are human. Healing is not a straight line. It is not a single breakthrough. It is a relationship with yourself that deepens over time.

The work you did here continues each time you pause, breathe, and listen inward. It continues when you speak to yourself with kindness instead of judgment. It continues when you notice a pattern and choose to respond rather than react. It continues when you allow even one small part of you to feel seen.

You chose to do this work, and that choice matters.

Let it matter to you.

Let it land.

Let it be enough for now.

Your journey does not end here.

You simply take the next step with more clarity, more compassion, and more connection than you had when you began.

Thank you for allowing me to walk alongside you in these pages.

I am grateful for your presence, your effort, and the honesty you brought to this work.

We continue together.

Author Note

Thank you for spending time with this Workbook and for allowing it to accompany you on part of your inner journey. Doing this kind of work asks you to slow down, turn inward, and meet yourself with honesty. That is never easy, and it deserves to be acknowledged. Your willingness to sit with your story, your parts, and your patterns speaks to a courage that often goes unseen.

I created this Workbook because I needed these tools myself. I am still learning, still listening to my own inner system, and still discovering places that ask for care and attention. This work is not theoretical for me. It is personal. It is ongoing. It continues to shape the way I live, the way I relate, and the way I understand the world. My hope is that these pages offered you structure, support, and the sense that you are not walking this path alone.

Your journey continues beyond here. Trust the process that brought you to this point. Trust the breath that steadies you. Trust the parts of you that carried you through the hardest seasons of your life and are still here, willing to walk with you into what comes next.

I am grateful you allowed this work to be part of your life for a little while. You carry the rest forward.

With respect and sincerity,

Keith W. Fiveson

Work Mindfulness Institute

www.ingramcontent.com/pod-product-compliance
Lightning Source LLC
LaVergne TN
LVHW081528060526
838200LV00045B/2037